WHY CAN'T I FIX IT?

The Questions We Ask When We Love Someone with Addiction

NATHAN DETERING

Skinner House
Boston

www.skinnerhouse.org

Printed in the United States

Cover design by Book Buddy Media
Text design by Tim Holtz
Author photo by Karyn Knight Detering

print ISBN: 978-1-55896-898-1
eBook ISBN: 978-1-55896-899-8

6 5 4 3 2 1
28 27 26 25 24 23

Library of Congress Cataloging-in-Publication Data

Names: Detering, Nathan, author.
Title: Why can't I fix it? : the questions we ask when we love someone with
    addiction / Nathan Detering.
Description: Boston : Skinner House Books, [2022] | Summary: "A resource
    for people who love someone who is dealing with addiction"-- Provided by
    publisher.
Identifiers: LCCN 2022032533 (print) | LCCN 2022032534 (ebook) | ISBN
    9781558968981 (paperback) | ISBN 9781558968998 (ebook)
Subjects: LCSH: Substance abuse--Social aspects. | Addicts--Family
    relationships.
Classification: LCC HV4998 .D48 2022 (print) | LCC HV4998 (ebook) | DDC
    362.29--dc23/eng/20220811
LC record available at https://lccn.loc.gov/2022032533
LC ebook record available at https://lccn.loc.gov/2022032534

"Anthem" by Leonard Cohen. Copyright © 1992 by Leonard Cohen, used by permission of The Wylie Agency LLC.

Table of Contents

Why Couldn't I Save Him?

Nick called me just as I was pulling into the church parking lot, my work day just beginning. I let the phone ring longer than I did for anyone else, letting my worry about my younger brother battle against my desire not to know what was wrong this time. The phone rang and rang. But worry won, as it always did, and so did hope—hope that maybe today would be the day I could say some marvelous word or magic phrase that would help Nick be honest with me and himself about his addiction and then ask for help. But today wasn't that day. All he wanted was to tell me how cool his new car was and how great the kids were at the school where he taught. His enthusiasm and upbeat mood almost lured me into pretending I didn't hear the ever-so-slight slur around the edges of his words.

"Good, Nick, good—um, hey," I said, hesitating, trying to figure out how to tell him what I was noticing without him shutting me out. I never quite learned how to walk that conversational tightrope, maybe because it isn't possible. "Hey, um, it sounds like you're slurring your words a bit. You take anything today?"

"No, no . . . I mean, the doctor gave me some new meds to help relax me a bit. You know I'm a worrier. You are too. All of us in our family are. Just trying to get the dose right. It's fine! I'm fine!"

"But, Nick—" I interrupted, my voice calm.

"Dude, give me a break, OK? I was just calling to say I'm doing well.

You asked me to check in, OK, so that's what I'm doing. But listen, I gotta go, class starting soon . . ."

Click, and then the dial tone.

I had fifteen minutes before my first pastoral appointment, which was maybe enough time to put the worrying about Nick, the wondering what to do, in a box to be opened later. Sometimes I could do it; sometimes I couldn't. Mornings like this weren't new. How many times did I sit in my car, outside the church where I have served as minister for the last sixteen years, having tightrope conversations like these with my brother? Too many, but never enough. How many times did I walk through the halls and rooms of the church and sit in the sanctuary, asking how I was supposed to love him, whether I was supposed to hold him tighter, or if I needed to let go? Too many, but never enough.

Because then, despite all my and my family's efforts and all our love, Nick died from an opiate overdose. He left behind a brokenhearted four-year-old son, a wife, students at the school where he was an assistant principal and teacher, parents, friends, a full future, and an older brother—me—who had marveled at the easy way Nick gained friends, joined the crowd, and always seemed to effortlessly capture the essence of cool. I wanted to be like him so much. If I had told him that more often, would it have made a difference?

Because I am a parish minister, it's easy for me to think I am supposed to have answers to my congregation's problems. Many factors push this expectation on me. Social location is one. I am a Unitarian Universalist, and although Unitarian Universalism has a long history of commitment to social justice principles, our congregations tend to be predominantly white, relatively wealthy, and often located in suburbs. We don't always do a good job of acknowledging the racial diversity that does exist among us, our members who are Black, Indigenous, and people of color, and we are often entangled in the elements of white supremacy culture that Tema Okun describes in her essay "White Supremacy Culture: Still Here." In particular, we tend to see ourselves as problem-solvers and as qualified to help others rather than as being in need of help ourselves. We celebrate personal success. These tendencies are so entrenched that a person can feel shame for not knowing an exit route from their struggles.

Theology is another. Unitarian Universalists have long celebrated the individual's ability to discern and decide for themselves their own theology. We choose our own names for the sacred, our own practices for spiritual growth, our own sources of religious authority. This liberty can be exhilarating, especially for people coming to us from traditions in which they did not feel able to be themselves or believe their own truths. But the Unitarian Universalist emphasis on self-reliance can be exhausting and leave us longing for mutual care and accountability. Our congregations can give us these, but sometimes we need to be reminded to focus more on covenanting together than on individual freedom.

And my role as minister often makes me hesitate to share my own doubts and worries. The robe and stole, the title of "Reverend" before my name, even the architecture of the church, with its rows of pews facing a high pulpit, set me apart from everyday congregants. I meet people who long for certainty in our uncertain world, who ask for help in discerning their life's purpose, who call on me to explain the inexplicable on behalf of God. In the face of such aching need, I feel pressed to show assurance.

Should I have prayed more for Nick? Never mind that I don't believe prayers can earn favors as a sort of quid pro quo. Why didn't I know how bad things had gotten for him? Never mind that Nick was a master at hiding his addiction from everyone, including himself. Why couldn't I save him? Never mind that I wasn't awarded the power of salvation along with my divinity school degree. I whisper at night: Why did God let this happen? Never mind that in our tradition we don't preach that God inscrutably decrees who lives and who dies.

I sometimes think it would be easier if I kept these midnight questions private. After all, it's pretty easy to hide grief and worry in my suburban white-majority culture, which emphasizes optimism and the ability to "get going" and "move on." But, since Nick died, something surprising has happened. Thanks to a generous congregation that hasn't asked me to pretend, and to our UU faith that teaches me that suffering is part of life, not punishment for a way of living, I'm learning to be present to the pain. I'm learning how communities, such as my congregation, can help one another respond to this pain together.

One outcome of my staying present to the pain is this book you hold in your hand. Preachers sometimes give sermons that we ourselves need to hear, and this book is one I have needed to read. It takes its shape from the tender, honest conversations I have had with people both in and outside my congregation who have shared with me their own stories of loving a family member with addiction. We asked each other the questions we had asked ourselves; we helped each other find answers to them. When I began speaking publicly about my experiences with addiction, I was surprised by how many people came to speak with me about their and their families' own experiences—but I should not have been. It was as if we just needed that first nudge of permission and encouragement to free ourselves from our culture's expectations, stop pretending, and start telling our truth.

Our need for a nudge to tell our addiction stories reflects the predominantly white suburban culture my congregation belongs to, which not only allows but expects us to hide our struggle with our loved ones. This is true even for people of color who are coping with addiction in their families; they are living in white supremacy culture, facing a double burden of addiction and racism. Still, my conversations with both people of color and white people illuminate important differences in their experiences, including in the ways addiction is responded to by law enforcement and talked about in faith communities. While I hope the wisdom gleaned from the interviews shared here will be helpful to all those struggling with addiction and its effects, it's true that its effects on me, my family, and members of my congregation reflect the particular culture we belong to. Does this mean this book is limited in scope? Absolutely. I recognize that a whole other book needs to be written that examines the intersectional impacts addiction has across people's spiritual and emotional lives. That being said, I am grateful for the conversations shared here because they have helped me unpack some of my assumptions about how addiction impacts us as family members.

I must confess that researching, interviewing for, and writing this book has been harder than I was prepared for. The stories I have heard brought back memories and resurfaced feelings I thought I had reckoned with or didn't even know I had. The perspectives I heard from people outside my community have revealed to me just how much my and my congregation's response to addiction has been shaped by whiteness and privilege. Much like the journey of companioning our loved ones in addiction crisis, the creation of this book has been a raw process marked with fresh sadness and fresh hurt. But it has also brought fresh hope.

Not long after Nick died, a friend shared with me a line from Hemingway's *A Farewell to Arms:* "The world breaks every one and afterward many are strong at the broken places." Addiction has broken so many families within our congregations and communities. It certainly broke mine. This book is about reckoning with that breakage, and then leaning into the work of helping the families in our communities get stronger at our broken places. I am glad that my Unitarian Universalist theology and spiritual practices can help us. In our congregation we light our chalice, we share our prayers of sorrow and joy, we come together in community to help us hold hope, we practice being the people the world and families need, we seek to establish the kingdom of Heaven here in this life instead of pinning our hopes on some other life, and we affirm that no one is beyond the reach of God's love. Whether you are a member of my faith, of another, or of none, I hope that you too will find healing and hope in these pages.

CHAPTER 1

Why Is This Happening?

When things get desperate we all reach for the support of something greater than ourselves. The Unitarian Universalist theologian Forrest Church says that "God is not God's name. God is our name for the mystery that looms within and looms beyond the limits of our being. Life force, spirit, ground of being, these too are names for the unnameable." But whatever name we give to that mystery, we cry out to it when things get bad. This is true whether or not we believe our cries are being heard. We cry out because when we're faced with addiction in our child, sibling, spouse, parent, or friend, we want to know why, and what now, and what next, and what to do.

I remember the first time I heard these questions up close. It was years before my brother's addiction issues got bad, but stories of opiate abuse were increasingly appearing in the news. One summer Saturday I found myself in the ER getting stitches in the palm of my hand after a bicycle repair went wrong.

"Yep, you cut yourself pretty good. Is your bike mad at you?" said the nurse as I showed her the sprocket-shaped crescent wound on my hand. "And look, you even have grease in there too! Well done." Knowing something of the challenges that her job brought, I didn't begrudge her sarcasm one bit.

But since my injury was deemed lower priority than the other needs in the ER that afternoon, I was left a while to wait. Outside the blue curtains drawn around the gurney I was sitting on I heard all kinds of unfolding emergencies: allergic reaction to bee stings across the hall; heart pain and shortness of breath reported matter-of-factly by an EMT to the doctor walking past; a woman cursing about the dog who broke loose from its leash, causing her to fall and break her wrist.

The stream of these voices was suddenly drowned out by the voice of a woman just on the other side of the curtain on my left. She sounded panicked, plaintive.

"Joey, what happened? They said they found you—"

"I'm sorry!" a voice said back, soft, ashamed.

"But what happened?

"I don't know, I just, I just . . . I didn't mean to. I'm sorry, mom."

"You took something?" Silence, perhaps a nodding head.

"What did you take? What did you take?" Silence again, but there must have been a whispered word.

"You used heroin? Joey, Joey—oh, God, Joey! Why?"

"I'm sorry, mom, I'm so sorry . . ."

"Oh, God," cried the mom.

Just then the nurse pulled back my curtain and said it was time for my stitches. The stabbing pinch of being sewn up was nothing compared to the pain I couldn't unhear on the other side of the curtain. I felt Joey's regret for the hurt he had caused himself and his mom. But even more, I felt his mother's fear as she was confronted, perhaps for the first time, with her son's drug use. I began imagining the questions she might ask in the days to come: Why did this happen? What am I supposed to do? What do I tell people? Did I do something to cause this? Is this my fault?

Thirty minutes later I was walking out of the hospital and leaving behind the unfolding emergencies in that day's ER. But ever since I have carried Joey's voice and his mom's voice with me, remembering them especially as my own brother began to struggle and I heard myself and my parents ask and ache with questions of our own. It's bad enough that most of these questions don't have answers. What's worse is how lonely it feels to ask them, each of them pinging around in our head and heart as we watch the people around us and think no one can possibly be feeling what we're feeling, what our family is feeling. Among the struggles that addiction brings are isolation, secrets, hushed stories, shame. Which is why it felt so healing to talk with Terry, the first person in my congregation with whom I discussed this question of "Why?"

Why do we ask why?
TERRY'S STORY

Terry and I don't need small talk to get into the real conversation we need to have. That's because we share a common language given us by the addiction history in our family stories. It wasn't always that way. For years Terry was part of the back-of-the-sanctuary crowd: coming into worship late and by himself, leaving as soon as it ended, only greeting me vaguely if I happened to be nearby and catch his eye as he came in. He politely refused our invitations to officially join the congregation and seemed happy to keep mostly to himself.

That changed after I shared with the congregation what had happened to my brother, speaking as transparently as I knew how about his addiction disease and his death from an overdose. I told them that I was committed to talking openly about an issue that is often kept hidden. The next Sunday, after service had ended, Terry was waiting for me at the end of the receiving line, ten feet behind everyone else. Coming close, he took my hand and looked directly into my eyes as he told me how sorry he was for me and my family. He also said that we had something in common, and that sometime he would like to tell me about his dad. We met over coffee several weeks later, and as his trust in me grew he began to share more about himself, his life, and his dad. Our conversations were of the unheralded kind that nonetheless fill our lives with grace.

On the day of our interview, Terry invites me into his small apartment. A middle-aged white man, he lives alone, his wife having died years ago and his children grown. Winter is blowing outside, but it is warm where we sit. We're relaxed even though the topic is painfully tender. Terry begins by asking me, "You know how when we're kids we assume that the world we live in is the only world? And we adapt to that. And we have these adaptive strategies to adapt to that crazy world. That's what I did." The first thing his dad would do after coming home from work, he says, was to drink an entire bottle of sherry.

"When was the first time you knew something was up with your dad's drinking?" I ask him.

"Well, we moved from one city to another, and I was nine or ten, and it just sucked. I remember him coming home from work and just starting drinking. And it was crazy, because even then I thought this was something that all dads must have done, drink an entire bottle of sherry before dinner. And I didn't think anything of it for a few years. I didn't have a problem with his drinking. The problem was with his behavior, okay? He never hit any of us, which is a miracle because his own father, my grandfather, hit him a lot. I think that even when he was drunk, he resolved he was never going to do that.

"But he was very violent to property. He would just go into these drunken rages at night. I would wonder if things at work or at home were setting him off. Was it the job? Was it us? Certain nights it was just horrible. It's traumatic remembering it now. It's a trauma. It burns still, sitting here."

Terry is well past fifty years old, and yet his face flushes as he says this, a visible sign of the pain he feels. I ask him, "Did you ask why this was happening, why your dad drank so much? What caused the drinking?"

"Well, it's a cliché, right, that this only happens to people who must do things to deserve it. I mean, isn't that why people say 'everything happens for a reason'? I don't believe that. But I do wonder, now—did we do something to instigate Dad's drinking? Did he not like being around us? I mean, I never doubted he really loved me . . . but I do think he didn't know how to love himself. And I wonder about that. I wonder why."

There is a long silence after Terry tells me that, a silence that feels loud as both of us wonder about these people in our lives—my brother, Terry's dad—who seemed to find it so hard to accept themselves, to love themselves. Was this why Terry's dad drank? Was this why my brother returned again and again to drugs and alcohol? Because they were ashamed of who they were? Yes? Maybe? Can we ever know for sure? That's the problem with asking why someone is suffering. One question keeps on leading to another, as if everything and everyone would be better if we *just knew why*. And when we can't figure out why, or what to do, we feel ashamed.

Shame

Terry says that he never really doubted his dad loved him, but he did wonder if his dad loved himself. We can't be certain that his father drank because he didn't love himself, but it's certain that his drinking made him ashamed, and it made his family ashamed.

"Here's the irony," says Terry. "That my dad felt ashamed of himself, and so he drank, and that made the shame worse, because he felt ashamed of his behavior and we did, too. I was embarrassed by him. So, while I don't think asking why he drank was helpful to me, I did feel so embarrassed. Which only made all this worse, and maybe made his drinking worse. Remember the rages I told you about?"

I nod.

"He broke all this furniture in our house; just destroyed it. Late at night we'd hear the breaking and the crashing. And for years we didn't say anything, really. Like I said earlier, we just kept all this broken furniture in the basement where no one would see it."

Terry looks out the window into the falling snow, and even though he has benefited from years of therapy to help him reckon with his father's alcoholism directly, that broken furniture hidden in the basement is a haunting symbol of the shame Terry's family felt about their dad's drinking, and the denial everyone practiced to avoid having to deal with it directly. The addiction, like the broken furniture, was kept hidden. Upstairs new furniture was installed, emotions were kept in check, accommodations were made, pretending was possible. But underneath the surface—in the basement, and in Terry's heart—the truth of how things really were was stored away.

"Sometimes I go back and talk to the twelve-year-old Terry," Terry says. "It's a whisper of sorts that, you know, it's not quite okay that my dad breaks furniture, drinks a bottle of sherry every night, and we don't talk about it. I tell the young version of myself that's not okay."

I ask him what it feels like to hear himself say that.

"Well, when you're a kid it's often so internal. It's all unconscious. And he was my dad! I loved him! And you're not supposed to feel embarrassed about your dad, to feel actually ashamed of your dad. So it makes sense that I kept all this buried, and the rest of us did too. The truth was just too painful."

Terry's words sound like a confession. His dad's drinking wasn't his fault, but I hear him wonder if he was supposed to have responded to it somehow: confronted it more, denied it less, faced the shame head-on. It feels good to remind him that back when all this was happening he was just a kid, and parents are supposed to take care of their kids, not the other way around.

———

Not long after Terry and I spoke I learned of a letter my brother had written to himself during one of his periods of recovery. He wrote of how hard he found it to love himself, and how drugs and alcohol helped him forget how much he was hurting. Reading the letter brought fresh discovery and fresh pain, and I wondered again if I could have said more, done more, reached out more to remind him just how loved he was. Would that have made a difference? Can our love for people in our lives, like my brother and Terry's dad, make up for love they can't muster for themselves? Questions like these ache for answers that just don't come. They also invite shame, and a contagion of guilt that gets passed from one person to the next.

Even though Terry and I know better, we feel personally responsible for the addiction in our families. I have since learned this tendency to individualize and personalize is one among many characteristics of white supremacy culture that harms us all. In "(Divorcing) White Supremacy Culture," Tema Okun describes other characteristics, all of them interconnected and mutually reinforcing: perfectionism, a sense of urgency, denial, quantity over quality, worship of the written word, the belief in the one "right" way, paternalism, either/or binary thinking, power hoarding, fear of open conflict, progress as defined by more, the right to profit, objectivity, and the right to comfort.

Kuhn's work helps me see how the urgency Terry and I have felt to answer "how can we fix the addiction in our families?"—and the shame we felt at not finding an answer—are not personal to us, but instead features of a culture that Kuhn says "targets BIPOC people and communities with intent to destroy them directly; and targets and violates white people with a persistent invitation to collude that will destroy their humanity."

How different might our experiences have been if instead of asking "How can I fix this?" we asked, "Who can help me?" Kuhn says it well: "We are strongest when we are allowed to be vulnerable—with ourselves and each other. White supremacy culture does not allow for vulnerability. And this is a tragedy for us all."

When we feel shamed and disgraced, we need to remember that all of us—my brother, Terry's dad, and the rest of us—need a little grace and encouragement to reach out to others rather than trying to go it alone. Because if desperation causes us to look beyond ourselves, and even if our cries of "Why?" and "What could I have done?" are met only with silence, I still remember that we are all in this together, participants in the web of life, all of us accountable to and for one another. No wonder, then, that both Terry and I felt better after sharing so deeply with each other. We ended up practicing the covenant we say together every Sunday: Love is the spirit of this church, and we dwell together in peace, seek truth in love, and help one another. It's too easy to forget the companionship our covenant promises us, especially when we have a loved one struggling with addiction and we feel obligated to explain or fix it. But my faith teaches me that we need not be trapped in guilt and shame. It reminds me that we aren't alone and don't have to manage alone; we come together in community to support and affirm one another. This is what I tell the people in my congregation. And whether or not you are one of them, whether you are a Unitarian Universalist or a member of some other faith (or faiths) or of none, in this book I tell it to you as well. All of us have worth and dignity, and all of us are loved, without limit, throughout our lives.

CHAPTER 2

The Differences Racial Identity Makes

In the last chapter we heard Terry describe how his father felt shame and drank as a result, which in turn made Terry feel ashamed. It was easy for me to assume that anyone in Terry's position would have felt shame; his experience matched so much of my own and those that others in my community have described. This is one way in which white supremacy culture gets expressed: the assumption that the experience of two white men in the suburbs is universal. But then I spoke with Rev. Dr. J. Anthony Lloyd, a Black pastor of the largest African American interdenominational Christian congregation in metro-west Boston. In the two hours we spent together, he helped me examine how the impact of addiction is shaped by the communities we are embedded in. Wanting to learn how these differences are felt by a colleague of color in my own tradition of Unitarian Universalism, I then secured an introduction to Rev. Leslie Takahashi, a multiracial parish minister serving one of our congregations in California. The work we do as clergy, of preaching, teaching, caring, and counseling in our communities, is similar, but the differences in how addiction has affected us and the families we serve are sometimes vast.

"It's all about the redlines"
A CONVERSATION WITH REV. DR. J. ANTHONY LLOYD

"Nathan! How you doing? You still there at First Parish in Sherborn? I wondered."

"Yes, I am! Yes, I am! Where have the years gone?" I answer, and immediately feel a need to apologize. I met Rev. Lloyd just as I started my ministry, eighteen years ago, and despite my promises to stay connected we haven't seen or spoken to each other since. It's easy to blame the long gap on the pressure of my parish work, but I was drawn to Rev. Lloyd as a young minister, when I was in need of a warm and generous mentor. Rev. Lloyd is such a person. Why did I let all this time go by? What has gotten in the way?

"Listen, J. Anthony," I say. "Can I just say I'm really sorry for not staying in touch—" But he doesn't let me finish.

"Oh, no, that road goes two ways!"

"I know," I say, "but the thing is . . . I remember, even from our one meeting, that you just *knew stuff*, and I really felt like I didn't. I mean, I still don't. And you told me to reach out for anything and now here it is—" I pause with embarrassment, because it's so long. "Eighteen years later."

This makes him laugh. "Well, now . . . okay, okay. So, tell me about this book you're working on now."

So I tell him about it, and about my brother, and about all the people in my family and my congregation who have, in ways spoken and unspoken, revealed the addiction stories they had long kept secret. That's the thing. They have been secrets, and holding them inside has been exhausting. So when we find ourselves in a space where it's safe to share, or even when we just can't hold them in any more, they pour forth.

"What was his name, your brother?" Rev. Lloyd asks, because this is what pastors and other helpers try to do: they remind us how the people we love have an identity that is bigger than their addiction, even if it's hard for those closest to them to see.

"Nick. Nicholas. He was seven years younger than me. Married. A dad. A teacher."

"I'm sorry." Rev. Lloyd offers to add our family to the prayer list on Sunday. He tells me his prayer list is long these days, because the trauma—he used that word *trauma*—of addiction is everywhere in his community.

I tell him that this is why I reached out to him: because I want to hear how the people in his town and his church think about and care for those with addiction and their families. I did so on the recommendation of a colleague who wondered if predominantly white, suburban communities like mine might be particularly likely to experience addiction as secrecy and shame.

"It's all about the redlines, about redlining," says Rev. Lloyd. In the 1930s, federal housing policy designated certain neighborhoods and towns as safe places for banks to issue loans, while others were deemed "high risk." Neighborhoods deemed the most desirable were shown in blue or green on the maps, while the "hazardous" ones were red. The color on the map was determined, in large part, by neighborhood demographics.

"Guess what color your church's town was?" Rev. Lloyd asks.

It's not hard to guess. "Blue," I say.

"Uh-huh, and guess what color my town was, over here?"

"Red." I know the answer only because of the antiracism work my congregation has done in recent years, trying to understand why the communities Rev. Lloyd and I live and minister in are so hyper-segregated. But he has known about redlines for years, partly because they have had such a significant effect on how addiction is talked about in his community.

"This is one of the differences these redlines have made," he says. "The difference is that in our town folk couldn't get home loans, businesses couldn't get business loans, so eventually it was rental property everywhere, or empty buildings everywhere. And guess what moved in? Liquor stores moved in, on all the corners, and drugs moved in, on the corners. Then when police started policing the drugs, policing the alcohol, everyone in the community—kids, parents, elders— would see houses raided or people arrested. It was everywhere; it was 'normal.' I'm talking decades ago this started, OK, but still the impact is here. Because the investment hasn't come back, OK? So what we have in our community aren't lots of grocery stores or coffee shops. What we have are community centers, churches, we've got a methadone clinic, we've got needle exchange clinics. Addiction treatment places are everywhere.

"And guess what? Folk just learn to live with it, exist with it. But we've all been sort of traumatized. So when I hear you talk about your brother and 'coming out of the shadows' with his story, and how talking about addiction is talking about things that have been kept secret, all I can think is how folk in our community don't have that experience at all, because in oppressed communities the culture is about survival, OK? And when it comes to addiction and drugs and alcohol, what helps us survive is we name it, we speak it, because if we don't our community won't survive."

There is a long silence.

"Shame is not on the table, OK, because everyone knows someone who is struggling with drinking or drugs. Everyone."

Despite the segregation imposed by redlining, everyone knows someone who is struggling with addiction. The difference is that in my community it is all too easy to hide these struggles away, while in Rev. Lloyd's community there is no choice other than to bring them out in the open. I ask about this difference, and rather quickly he gets theological.

"Listen, there is a strand in some African American communities that says addiction isn't a health issue; it's a sin issue, along the lines of an inability to control oneself. These are the harmful theological attitudes that get shared around a bit. But I counter that in the pulpit with what I call Compassionate Grace, which is to say that God uses the medical field, doctors, treatment centers, churches, AA, et cetera to help all of us participate in our healing and restoration. We have to do our part as pastors, community members, family members to help each other confront our struggles. Our job as people, you see, is to tarry with folk and not to run or shun."

"Not run or shun. I like that," I say. I'm struck by how Rev. Lloyd uses the pulpit to respond to how addiction is affecting his community. I began preaching about it only after my own personal loss. Though addiction is endemic in our country, the capacity—and pressure—in predominantly white and affluent communities to deny and hide it has meant that my and my congregation's ministry has only recently trained our preaching and public witness upon it. Rev. Lloyd, however, has preached on addiction throughout his career because the question of how to *tarry with*, or abide with, people with addiction is known and named in his communities. The reasons for this difference intersect across race, racism, class, economy, zoning, and history, but for Rev. Lloyd the response to the families affected can and should be theological.

"The church's responsibility to come alongside these families, to tarry with them, is my language," he explains. "Remember when God asks Moses, when Moses is doubting himself, 'What's in your hand?' Moses had a staff, right? And what we've got in our hands in the church and as pastors is presence, is this ability to abide. Here's what we say: This is not who God made your spouse, child, parent to be, OK, someone struggling with addiction. We help them dream again, tell them how the dream they have for the person with addiction is deferred but not dead, give them this idea that they will get restored eventually.

"I said to my folk this past Sunday, referencing the scripture that talks about the enslavement of Egypt and the journey toward the Promised Land: as Black folk we're always going in and out of Egypt: slavery, the Civil War, the civil rights movement, and all that's happened in the last few years with George Floyd and Black Lives Matter. I feel we're always going in and out of Egypt, moving toward promised restoration but then moving back toward the bonds of Egypt. But as African Americans we have a history and a theology that says we stick at it, we tarry, we abide."

Listening to him, I feel that redlining has also divided our theological frameworks from each other. Unitarian Universalist theology is so often centered on individualism and personal explorations of belief, rather than on the community. Our national organization, the Unitarian Universalist Association, recently issued a significant report, *Widening the Circle of Concern*, that underlines our need to shift our theology away from the individual and toward covenantal relationship. "If freedom and individualism are our most important values, we have little to offer in these times," it warns. "These times require a liberatory faith that invites us each into the spiritual work of empathy and healing. . . . We need to put greater emphasis on what it means to be bound to one another in an interdependent web."

Rev. Lloyd offers just such an invitation. His call to "tarry" with folk in his community as they journey toward restoration is "urgent," he says. "Look, there is so much of what I call 'collateral damage' from addiction in these families, OK? One is the loss of a generation of wealth. So if the parent is struggling with addiction, and they lose their job or, even more common, they get put in prison for something related to their addiction, it's not just them that pays the consequences. It's the extended family that pays too, so I've seen folk lose houses, lose the income from their household's primary earner, OK? Or say the person in their household needs help, but the family doesn't have the resources to get them into treatment centers, or the family doesn't have the resources to welcome them back, which means the person is just stuck going in and out of detox centers or prison with no real path toward getting better. And if they do end up in prison, I mean . . ."

He pauses and sighs. "We've lost a whole generation of Black men in particular. A broad swath of our Black men are wiped out and put in a system where there is almost no rehabilitation, where substance use is easy to come by, where men are serving sentences for drug offenses that are often longer than for white collar crime.

"But listen: most of all, what all this just creates are just these norms of poverty and addiction that get rooted in families, which then send out tentacles across the community, in our collective economic health, in our mental health, in our spiritual health. Addiction never just happens to the individual. It happens to the community. And so, I tell my folk, we don't have the opportunity to run and shun. We need to tarry."

––––

As my conversation with Rev. Lloyd finished, I realized something had shifted. It wasn't just an interview anymore; I felt like I was in church, listening to a sermon I needed to hear. It is in religious community that we get the spiritual resources we need, and as a white minister serving in predominantly white spaces, I needed to hear how much deeper and different the collateral damage of addiction is in communities of color, as a result especially of racist housing policies and the criminalization of addiction. I needed to hear that secrecy, guilt, and shame weren't just personal or family responses to my brother's addiction; they were born of a culture my congregation and I are embedded in that frames our addiction experiences as individual failures, problems that should be dealt with in isolation rather than in community. As a leader in a predominantly white, middle-class denomination, I especially needed to hear how this work of "tarrying with" the families of people with addiction is spiritual work. It is the congregation's ministry over time to come up alongside these families and help them walk toward restoration.

The differences that redlines have made for the families in Rev. Lloyd's and my communities aren't unique to those communities; they exist everywhere and affect every family's response to addiction. Those of us who are acculturated to extreme individualism must work to move the conversation away from the individual and toward the community. "We need to see one another as partners," Rev. Lloyd told me at the end. He was speaking about the two of us, but he also was offering a new word for the families who feel they must cope alone with the damage that addiction has caused, and who need something new from their community: *partnership*.

"Becoming one of the mourners"
A CONVERSATION WITH REV. LESLIE TAKAHASHI

Sometimes it's good to begin at the end. At the end of our conversation, I ask Rev. Leslie Takahashi what she wants to tell a person who is reading this book because of addiction in their family. She replies immediately, because sometimes the truth doesn't need much reflection to come out.

"Two things: One, no matter what is going on with you or your loved ones, or what you may think you have or haven't done, you are still worthy of dignity and respect. And two, no matter how isolated or lonely you may feel, you are not alone."

"It feels so good to hear that, Leslie," I tell her, because even though I am writing this book, not reading it, I'm writing it because I too need to hear her message. Even after years of therapy, good spiritual counsel from beloved colleagues, and prayer, I still catch myself feeling that I'm carrying the burden of my brother's loss alone, and that my inability to "save" him says something about my worth as a sibling, a minister, or even a person. Where does this come from?

"Lots of places," says Rev. Takahashi. "Our culture tells us that we're supposed to be self-sufficient and capable, able to 'make things right.' Unitarian Universalism, in particular, tends to favor a rational, intellectual approach to the world. But we can't think ourselves into solving our loved one's addiction. So we feel shame, we feel guilt. And if we're not able to come forward and lay out what's hurting us, then the shame and guilt get compounded. Some religious traditions have practices like confession and altar calls that enable people to share their struggles, but in general our culture doesn't support people in acknowledging their helplessness and asking for help, whether from God or from other people."

"Preach," I tell her, because the best sermons are those that name something we have long felt but haven't quite put into words.

Rev. Takahashi comes to this perspective not just as a UU minister with decades of experience, but also as the daughter of an alcoholic and the mom of a child experiencing addiction. "My dad was an alcoholic, sometimes he was violent, and so much of his addiction came out of his experience as a Japanese American citizen forced into an internment camp in WWII, the trauma of what was said and done to him, the racism. And here's the thing: I never really did the work to understand how all of that got passed down to me—how his experience of racism, an experience that led to his addiction, ended up shaping me.

"I learned from my dad's experience of racism, what was said and done to him, that the world wasn't safe. His alcoholism, and especially his violence, made this learning viscerally true for me. So when I became a parent, because I didn't really do the work to understand how all this impacted me, I ended up passing down this codependent behavior to my kids, this feeling that it wasn't enough to just love them, that instead I had to create this perfect world for my kids. I was overprotective, over-careful, and I think I transmitted— from my dad and then through me—that the world wasn't safe. I feel like this ended up making my child susceptible to addictive behavior, because if they think the world sucks anyway, then why not just go ahead and try whatever, do whatever."

I've learned how addictive behavior gets passed down from one generation to the next. Indeed, there is increasing evidence that addiction has a genetic component. But Rev. Takahashi illuminated for me how her father's experience of racism became the catalyst for the addictions that followed. The world isn't as safe as any of us might want to believe, but the racism that Rev. Takahashi's multiracial family experienced made their world more and differently dangerous than it has been for me as a white person.

"The reality is that there is a correlation between systematic dehumanization—which is what racism does, it dehumanizes people—and addiction. The inherited trauma of racism means it doesn't get talked about, but it does get felt, it does get experienced, and that pain can lead to all kinds of places."

For Rev. Takahashi these places are profoundly personal.

"When I say I didn't do the work, I guess what I mean is that I didn't really understand how my experience as my father's daughter shaped my parenting. All I wanted to do was protect my children, okay, because of what I went through. So when my child began to suffer with addiction, it was just heartbreaking. I felt just utter despair that I wasn't able to protect my child, that I was powerless to solve my child's addictions, because isn't that my one job?"

Meanwhile, of course, Rev. Takahashi was (and still is) a multiracial person in a predominantly white community, serving as a parish minister in a culture and a religious tradition suffused with the myth of self-sufficiency. She never heard or saw anyone talking about what she was going through.

"The inherited trauma of racism doesn't really get talked about. Addiction doesn't really get talked about. I felt just so alone. So I did what I knew I could as a minister: I became public about my experience."

"And?" I ask, knowing something about the fear and also the relief that comes with doing that.

"And . . . we'll see! What I'm trying to create is a culture of asking for help. We as Unitarian Universalists aren't good at creating these kinds of cultures of asking for help. I keep saying over and over that talking about our suffering and asking for help is a gift we can give to our community, because others can learn, from our asking for help, how to break the silence and the myth of self-sufficiency."

I want Rev. Takahashi to be my minister. I tell her so as our conversation ends, and I ask about her child, who is in recovery.

"It depends. I'm living in the world of Both/And. I'm sad I don't have my child back as they once were . . . and I celebrate that I get another day with them. Hope springs eternal."

———

I spoke with both Rev. Dr. J. Anthony Lloyd and Rev. Leslie Takahashi during the second year of the COVID-19 pandemic, when all of us were experiencing forms of lockdown and isolation. Rev. Takahashi reminded me that more than a hundred thousand people also died from addiction-related causes in 2021. "These folk are us," she said.

My conversations with both these clergy of color have revealed how much our definition of "us" affects how we, as individuals and as communities, experience and respond to addiction. Communities of color may confront it more directly than white-majority ones because decades of structural racism, including redlining and other destructive policies, have meant that their members have easy access to addictive substances and few resources available for rehabilitation and recovery. The generational traumas of racism accumulate. White-majority families and communities are more likely than those of color to feel that their struggles must be hidden, and to suffer and feel shame in silence, but they too pass down their own familial trauma. And the genetic component of addiction is another way in which these struggles can descend from grandparent, to parent, to child.

I feel profoundly humbled by how much I still have to learn about racism's impact on addiction. It is important for more of us to go public with our addiction experiences, both in our communities and beyond them. Rev. Lloyd and Rev. Takahashi are showing the way.

CHAPTER 3

What Can You Do?

If I had found this book when Nick was in the throes of his addiction, this would have been the first chapter I turned to. Those of us trying to love someone who is actively using are desperate for answers, direction, ideas, and support as we try to figure out how to help them. So let's get this hard truth out of the way first: there are things that we as family and friends can do to help our sibling, parent, child, spouse, or friend recover from addiction. And sometimes they just aren't enough. There is no sure-fire fix. But that doesn't mean we are helpless.

The words you can say

One weekday morning a couple years before Nick died, our mom left me a voicemail. Even before listening to the message I was worried, because back then she never called during the workday. She was calling to ask if I had heard from Nick. Would I please call her back as soon as possible? "I don't think he's doing well," she said. "We haven't heard from him all weekend."

My brother at this point was a grown man—he had a job and a child and a marriage—but a parent worries about their child, no matter how old the child is or how responsible they seem. It's been said that a child is a parent's heart walking around outside their body, unguarded and vulnerable. This is especially true when the child is leaning over the edge, telling everyone and maybe even himself that he's fine, just fine, but actually losing himself more and more to the drugs he is using to forget how he really feels about himself.

"Can you try calling him, too?" my mom says when I call back, and her voice is so fragile and cracked that I don't know who I want to crawl through the phone and wrap my arms around more, my brother or her.

"Right away," I say. This is what the rest of our family does, because of our love for Nick: we to try to protect, to rescue, to make things right, to ease the worry. That none of us feel equipped for this work, and that the disease of addiction can make success impossible, doesn't make the urge to do it any weaker.

But this time, I promise myself, I'll try a new approach. Elaine, the therapist I've been seeing, has been helping me discover how to take care of myself while also trying to take care of others. So this time I'll try to tell Nick honestly what I see happening with him, even though the conversation will be hard. Elaine has invited me to try telling him three things: how much I love him; that, because I love him, I need him to know how concerned I am about his drug use and how I see it affecting both him and everyone around him; and that I'm here in any and every way to help him get the help he needs.

When Elaine outlines these steps—in the safe, calm space of her comfortable office—they sound so damn easy. However, part of girding myself to have this conversation with Nick is figuring out what to do with the anger I feel. Everyone talks about the love we have for people like Nick, but what about the anger? It mixes with love in confusing ways. My affection for his easygoing charm and remarkable ability to connect with his students clashes with my bitterness at how his drug use fuels terrible choices, how he puts everyone—his son and wife, our parents, me and our sister, and his best self—second to finding the next high. Yes, addiction is a disease, but its symptoms can hurt and infuriate everyone around the person it grabs hold of. I guess this is one way that addiction becomes a family disease.

Elaine has a suggestion for this, too, but she says it will require some strength. She wants me to note the anger and name it, instead of letting it fly at him red-faced and untamed. She says Nick won't be able to hear my anger until he is well enough to take it in. But anger never feels so controlled. This is where my strength will be needed. So before I call, I do a lot of deep breathing. I don't want to let my anger overwhelm the words of love I want to share.

How many times does a brother let the phone ring before hanging up? Three, four, seven? How about ten? Halfway through the tenth ring, Nick picks up.

"Nate, hey," he answers, his voice hushed, rough, sleepy.

"Hey," I say, but before I can even begin my carefully prepped script he is already launching into a regretful apology.

"I know I need to call Mom and Dad. She asked you to call, right? I know. I called my sponsor today."

"You did? I mean, that's great." I'm surprised to hear this, and my relief is mixed with doubt because we've been here before. But I try to keep those feelings in the background, remembering what Elaine said. "Nick, listen. I just—I need you to know I love you, we love you and I'm worried about you."

"Yeah, I know," and even though I can't see him I can hear he is starting to cry. Will this breakdown be the one that leads to a breakthrough? Will this be the time recovery happens "for real" (whatever that means)? Is this the "rock bottom" (whatever that means) that addicts supposedly have to reach before they can begin recovering? But Elaine has taught me to steer away from such thinking. The future is now, she says. What matters is this moment here and now with Nick, not whether this is the moment that leads to everything changing.

Addiction doesn't work like that, she reminds me every time I see her. OK.

So I say, "I'm really proud of you for calling your sponsor. When are you going to a meeting? Do you need a ride? Can I help you get there? What can I do?" I know I'm asking too many questions, but I can't help it. It's like he's let me come close to him on the ledge and he's given me his hand and I see a chance to pull him back toward safety.

Which is what happens. After that call his sponsor did take him to a meeting. The meeting led to him sitting down to talk with our parents. That talk led to Nick telling us and himself that he needed more help than we or his sponsor could give. That acknowledgment led to a month in a treatment center. That time in treatment led to months of recovery. That recovery led to reconnection with his wife and son: afternoon trips for ice cream, games of Lego on the floor with his boy, and family dinners. That reconnection led to some reckoning with the truth, which then led to some honest conversations between Nick and me when I could tell him about my love . . . and my anger, too.

That the recovery didn't last forever doesn't make the time Nick spent connecting with all of us who loved him any less real. That the recovery didn't last forever doesn't make the honest conversations we had disappear. That the recovery didn't last forever doesn't mean my telling him I loved him and was worried about him didn't make a difference. Because when the relapse happened and Nick drew closer again to the edge, at least he knew I loved him. At least he could hear my voice telling him that. At least he knew I was there.

The places that can help
A CONVERSATION WITH ISAAC

Rush hour traffic has blocked the highway for miles, making me late for my in-person meeting with Isaac. So at the next service island I pull over and call him. I haven't met Isaac, I don't even know Isaac; I heard about him from Chip, a member of my congregation who attends a Narcotics Anonymous meeting with him, and who said he might be interested in speaking me with about this book project. After a couple texts and an email in which I explain this book project, Isaac says he would love to talk to me. It's as though it doesn't matter that we're strangers, because we belong to the same family: the addiction family. We don't need to know each other, or even have much in common, to tell each other our stories, without pretense or self-protective BS. I hate the reason Isaac and I are able to have this kind of intimacy, but I cherish the intimacy itself. Nothing, it seems, about this reckoning with addiction is without some contradiction.

"Hello? This is Isaac. Pastor Nathan?" Isaac's voice fills the car, his West Indian accent still bright despite the thirty years he has lived in the States. I am eager to talk with him because I know how important he has been for Chip's recovery. Chip's story is a hopeful counterpoint to the many stories of relapse and loss; he has been clean for twenty years. (The term "clean" is commonly used, but I admit I find it problematic; does it imply that those who aren't sober are "dirty"?)

I tell Isaac that, although he may not know it, he's a lifeline for this member of my church.

"Well, it wasn't always that way," Isaac says. And then he describes his own love affair with substances, how growing up in the era of "sex, drugs, and rock and roll" meant that getting high one way or another was "just the thing, you know? It was what we did, looking forward to having a drink or a joint or whatever it was, and it was good . . . until it wasn't."

As a young man Isaac emigrated to the States, married, served in the military for a couple years, had children, went to school, and began a successful career as an engineer. On the outside he was thriving. But on the inside he had a secret.

"It got to the point where other, harder drugs came in, you know . . . and it became very, very expensive. I mean, I worked a lot then, I have four kids! I was a good dad! But I would get paid on Thursdays and it got to happen that I was spending so much on my drugs that a week later I was scratching for pennies. So that was the first sign to my family that something was wrong. And then I started to miss some work days here and there. I mean, my work never really slacked off, but I would use my vacation days or sick days to kind of recover from my drug use. And it became obvious to everyone there was a problem."

So far, Isaac's story parallels Nick's: good times slowly turning into something else, achieving professional and personal success while keeping the growing addiction hidden, living a life divided between the healthy successes on the one hand and the addictions on the other. Where they part ways is what happened next.

"You know what the most important conversation in my recovery was?" asks Isaac. And I'm thinking: the one he had with his wife where he came forward and told her the truth? Or the one where he told his children, who are always more aware of what's going on at home than they get credit for?

"It was when I went into work and met with Anne from the human resources department, who I sometimes took lunch breaks with. And maybe because I didn't know what else to do, or because I was desperate to keep my job, I just . . . told her everything that was going on. Everything."

"Wow. I mean, weren't you scared you would lose your job or get in trouble?" Isaac can't see my face, but I think he hears the surprise in my voice. The story I am familiar with would have Isaac, like Nick, hiding what is really going on from his employer, faking it to make it, living a divided life. And while I know addiction doesn't discriminate according to race or gender or class, I also know that institutions and people do discriminate in how they respond to those with addiction. Nick was a white professional, and his drug use landed him in recovery clinics. When people of color use drugs, whether they're professionals or not, they often land in prison. This is the system in which Isaac, a Black immigrant man, was living when he was honest with Anne about why he missed days at work and used up all his vacation long before the year was out. It was risky.

"But listen, Nathan, I was desperate. I needed help. I loved my job. I wanted to come clean. And you know what she said?" Isaac's voice is still marveling and full of gratitude these twenty years later. "I'll never forget it. She said, 'Isaac, you're one of our best. You will have a lot of people pulling for you.' And then she wrote down the address of a church near my home where there was a Narcotics Anonymous meeting every Tuesday night. I went the next week and I haven't missed a Tuesday since. I have been sober ever since."

I know from experience that it could have been otherwise for Isaac. I know from my experience with Nick that NA and AA and church basements with stale but free coffee and worn podiums at which people say their names and tell their stories aren't for everyone. I know from my experience that not everyone meets someone like Anne in the HR department; instead they may meet horrified eyes or company policy or vague waves of the hand that tell someone like Isaac to come back when he's got his life together (if he gets to come back at all).

But that doesn't mean Isaac's story isn't important to share. Because in Anne's office, and in that church basement every Tuesday night, and then, later, in the sanctuary where Isaac began attending worship every Sunday, and in the kitchen where his family gathered for dinner most nights, here's what Isaac found: he found a community of people who, in Anne's words, were pulling for him.

"One of the first Sundays I went to church the pastor began reading Hebrews 11. You know, the one that says 'faith is the evidence of things hoped for, the assurance of things not seen.' I heard that and felt like the pastor was talking straight to me, saying that folks around me had faith in my recovery, had assurance that I could get better even if none of us could see it yet."

The good news I'm hearing from Isaac is that such places and such people and such faith exist. In the midst of my loss of Nick and the numb resignation that sometimes swamps me, I notice how much I am leaning on Isaac's story. He needed the faith that others had in him to help him get through. I need the faith that sometimes the person working to recover, the recovery meetings they find or are guided to, and the community that forms around them make all the difference. In the midst of my feelings of helplessness and angst, Isaac's story offers something like hope.

I need you to see me, even if it hurts
BETH'S REQUEST

For as long as I've served as her minister, I've known Beth was a recovering alcoholic. She seems to hold this part of herself with lightness, sharing it in meetings or social settings with an ease that has the remarkable effect of normalizing a topic that for many people is tender or even taboo. Case in point: Once, in the drink line at a church event, the guy in front of us offered her a glass of wine.

"Oh, no, thank you!" Beth says. "Just seltzer and lemon, please."

"What, you don't drink?" he says, sounding almost offended. Some folks seem to take other people's abstinence as a personal affront, as a criticism of them and their choices. This is one place where the peer pressure to drink or use begins, and it takes some self-assurance to risk disappointing or angering the people around us so that we can stay true to ourselves. An important part of helping someone in recovery is helping them learn to love themselves more than they want acceptance from others.

Beth has become a person who loves herself that much. I know this because she says back to the man, with not a hint of defensiveness but all the self-confidence in the world, "No, I'm an alcoholic. I haven't had a drink in fifteen years. But I love seltzer and lemon!"

And the man, startled at her openness, and maybe also ashamed of his question that was almost an accusation, says awkwardly, "Oh . . . um, gosh, sorry, Beth! I mean, good for you! Can I get you that seltzer then?"

"Yes, thank you! And don't apologize, OK? Next time I'm buying you a drink." And he laughs a weak, relieved laugh as he hands her the seltzer. So much of Beth's self-awareness about her addiction, and the pressure on her to keep it secret, is captured in a moment like this. Since then she and this man have served on committees together, sharing the work of the church community. Her refusal to treat her addiction as shameful, something to be hidden, helps him and others to see her as a full person, with all her capability and worth.

My family and I worried and dithered about how, when, where, even *whether* to talk openly about our addiction story. So much of the shame that addiction brings in predominantly white, suburban communities like ours—and

Beth's—is driven by our view of it as a personal failure. "She can't handle her drink!" we mutter—or we fear that someone else will mutter. "They let themselves go!" "He didn't know when to stop!" But the truth is that drug and alcohol use and abuse occur in the context of our communities, families, and identities, and I'm struck by how Beth acknowledges this.

"You have to understand," she says, "just how much my identity as a white middle-class woman has played into my alcoholism. Alcohol is integral to the country club set, cocktail parties are what you do, martini lunches are a thing, and if it's a bit too much no one says anything—at least not publicly.

"I saw drinking as part of being a grownup. I came from a family where all the adults around me had at least one or two drinks every night. I remember looking forward to the day I could sit at a bar and have a drink. That felt like an important rite of passage, the way I could see myself and be seen by others as having arrived."

So that's what Beth did. She started drinking at fourteen, stolen sips here and there when no one was looking, and then on the weekends as part of the high school party circuit, and then even more in college, when her roommate sometimes found her blacked out in the snow, and then all by herself in her apartment after college, one glass of wine turning into the whole bottle, night after night. Beth didn't stop until she was twenty-seven.

"About this time I was diagnosed with a mental health condition, and I realized during the treatment that I had been self-medicating for years, that I was using alcohol to stuff emotions down so that I wouldn't have to deal with them or learn from them."

Beth didn't do anything about her drinking right away, but one morning after waking up to what she describes as "empty wine bottles from last night around me and fogged memories of crying uncontrollably but not knowing why," she decided she needed help. She went, with a friend, to the first AA meeting she could find. It's a decision that many people never make. At meetings Beth found support that also pushed her to be accountable for her drinking, and as the treatment for her mental illness began to take hold, she was able to string one day of sobriety into another and another. She hasn't had a drink since.

Beth's recovery seems smoother than some. What was harder was telling her family and having them dismiss her.

"I remember my parents coming out. I was sixty days sober, and they came to visit. We were sitting out at a restaurant near the ocean and everybody got a beer—my dad, my mom got a beer, and I didn't. And I remember them sort of, like, 'Hey, what's going on?' And I said, you know, 'I'm not drinking anymore.' And they were both kind of, like, 'You? Why? You don't have a drinking problem!' I mean, they just kept trying to tell me that I was fine, that I was taking things too far, that I'm okay, that everything's okay. But I wasn't okay, and they just didn't want to hear that.

"I've thought a lot about why that was. They are loving parents, and I'm sure part of their response was wanting to reassure me. But I also wonder if what was at stake for them, in accepting what I was telling them, was upsetting their status quo: the status quo that meant they didn't need to think about their own drinking; the status quo that says they aren't the kind of people who have an alcoholic daughter; the status quo that says they don't bear any responsibility, whether it's genetic or situational or social, for their daughter being a drunk. I don't really think they thought it was possible that this would happen to their daughter. They thought that it *couldn't* be possible, having come from the family I come from."

But of course it's possible. The context and culture Beth grew up in might even have made it more likely. Which is why Beth's plea to her parents at the end of that meal cuts so deep and so true: "Look, I just need you to see me, okay, even if it hurts. If you can't, I just need you to leave me alone."

Beth made that request of her parents more than twenty years ago, and she says that she still has to remind them that she remains an alcoholic even though she hasn't had a drink in more than two decades. Her story leaves me even more impressed by her response to the man in the drink line who seemed threatened by her sobriety. "Oh, I'm an alcoholic; haven't had a drink in twenty years, but I love seltzer and lemon!" She made it sound so easy, so light. But beneath her words is the work she continues to do of accepting herself, and asking others to do the same.

———

When I remember Nick's addiction story and listen to stories from both in and outside my congregation, like Isaac's and Beth's, I can't help longing to find a magic formula, a clear series of steps we can take to assure our loved one's recovery. That longing never goes away, even though I know these things don't exist. Each person is different, their addictions and what drives them are complex, and what works for some doesn't work for others. But these stories do reveal some practices that are likely to be helpful.

First, we remember my therapist Elaine's urging to say three things to our loved one. We should tell them how much we love them, and tell them that, because we love them, we need them to know how concerned we are about their substance use and how we see it affecting them. And we should tell them we are here, in any and every way, to help them get the help they need.

Second, from Isaac we remember there are people and communities who may have even more faith in our loved one's recovery than they do. We learn that telling the truth to someone, as Isaac did to Anne from human resources, can begin a chain of events that leads to health. And we learn that recovery programs like Narcotics Anonymous and Alcoholics Anonymous can offer the supportive accountability that our loved one needs.

Third, from Beth we learn that if our loved ones confide in us about the depth of their struggles, we need to not dismiss or minimize what they are telling us. This is especially true when their addiction scares us or makes us worry that we contributed to it in some way. When we're tempted to respond with defensiveness and denial—and we will be—we need to take a breath and find other places and people who can help us with our feelings, instead of unloading them on our loved one. This might mean attending a support group for family members of alcoholics or drug users (such as Al-Anon) or speaking with a therapist, a member of the clergy, or a friend. Our loved one needs us to be with them and listen to them, but we can only do that if we too are getting the support we need.

Will any of this work for you? Maybe yes, maybe no. The frustrating—and heartbreaking—reality is that each person's recovery is unique, personal, and ultimately dependent on them. However, these practices offer something we as family and friends don't often feel with our loved one's addiction: steps to take, a path forward, and a place where hope can grow.

CHAPTER 4

What Can't You Do?

Earlier in this book I've mentioned Tema Okun's insightful writing on white supremacy culture. One feature of white supremacy culture that's particularly relevant here: perfectionism. "Perfectionism," Okun says, "is the belief that we can be perfect or perform perfectly." It includes the presumption that we can demand that others be perfect as well as expecting perfection of ourselves. Perfectionism shows up in a host of ways. For instance, we tend to see mistakes as personal, as reflecting badly on the person who made them. We leap to identify what's wrong with something or someone but are less able to appreciate what's right. And we do this to ourselves, as well; we carry harsh critics within ourselves, focusing on our faults and "failures." We internalize standards we did not set and then blame ourselves for not meeting them.

This is directly relevant to how families are impacted by a loved one's addiction. We are held up to an impossible standard of competency, expected—and expecting ourselves—to be able to help our loved one recover. And when we can't, because our loved one's recovery isn't up to just us, the inner critic is ready to find fault and tell us we've failed.

In my family, we felt not only that we were losing the best parts of Nick to his addiction, but also that we were losing our sense of ourselves as people who could and should be able to make a difference to him. Not only were we were losing him, we were also losing our self-image as doers, solvers, helpers—as people who could save him. Our inner critics had a field day with my family.

What I've learned since then, both from Okun's work and from therapy, is that there is no perfect way to help our loved ones toward recovery. And it's not our job to find one. Loving is our job: loving honestly and tenderly enough to tell our loved one with addiction the truth, and loving in a way that lets us accept the limits to what we can do to help them recover. It's heartbreaking and freeing work, all at the same time.

We did everything
A CONVERSATION WITH MOM

At the end of one of our recent phone conversations, my mother told me, "If you still want to talk with me about your book . . . we can. I will." She said it so fast, almost doggedly, that I wasn't sure if I'd heard her correctly. Months earlier I'd asked if we could talk about Nick and what his addiction struggle was like for her as his mom, and after a few days' silence she'd said she was sorry, but she couldn't. "I'm proud of the work you're doing, I know it will help people, but I . . . just can't." The terrible ache in her voice revealed the dilemma she felt, wanting to help one son with his project but not wanting to sink again into the gaping emptiness of the other son's loss. Immediately I regretted asking her. Months went by and nothing was said. Some things are just too tender to touch. But now she had brought it up again, out of nowhere.

"Are you sure?" I asked. "Because back in the spring you said you just couldn't, that it was too hard. It's really okay. I understand."

"Yes. I want to." She said it firmly, and I knew better than to ask what had changed. Some things are too tender to touch, but the ache was there whether she spoke of it or not; she awoke to Nick's loss every day. "It's not like a wound," she said, "but like a hole that has no bottom and never gets filled."

Not all conversations are easier over the phone, but this one was. At least the sun was shining in the backyard where I was sitting, her voice coming in stereo through my earbuds as I stared at the blooming blue hydrangeas and caught the scent of the nearby potted basil. If we were sitting together it would be too easy to talk about the hydrangea, the basil. Small talk would tempt us to avoid the tougher topics. I also can't bear seeing her cry.

Tears are where my mom begins our conversation—not with her own tears, but by telling me about Nick's. "I did everything I knew how to do—coaching him, sending him to counseling, giving him money for rehab, rushing in, pulling back, giving him advice, when he asked for it, about how to hang onto his job and his marriage. And when that wasn't working, I would just hold him in my arms and let him cry until he couldn't cry anymore."

I wasn't expecting this picture of Nick plaintive and desperate about his addiction, rather than defiant or defensive. When he talked to me I always wondered if he was only telling me what I wanted to hear, but with our mom his guard was down, all his needs laid bare for her to see.

"He would ask me, 'Can I come live at home if I need to?' Of course, I would say without hesitation, even though I was hesitating. 'Can I give you all the prescription bottles? I don't trust myself with them.' Yes, I would say, even though I felt nervous about having them. 'Will you go to the doctor with me? I want you there to help me tell him I don't just want to get prescribed more pills.' What time? I would say, even though I felt such anger at the doctor for prescribing the pills again and again.

"He tried everything. We tried everything. But his addiction demons were like a big knot of fishing wire, and we just didn't know where to start pulling to untangle it. But we kept trying, pulling here, tugging there . . . because you can never do enough. He was my baby boy."

For the first time, she shares with me her memories of the last day of Nick's life, telling me how she spoke with him that morning. They made plans for him to go to my parents' house in the evening to have dinner and watch the baseball game, something they did together almost every week, no matter how good or bad things were. Routines like this can be a life-line when everything else is uncertain.

But—and this is so hard to hear my mom say—"he never came. He died from the overdose sometime that afternoon. And I keep thinking, even now, four years later: was there anything that could have been different that day? Did I hear anything different in his voice? Should I have noticed something? Should I have gone over earlier? What if?" She asks again and again, "What if?" with her voice trailing off into a whisper.

It's understandable—and heartrending—that we end-lessly, helplessly rehearse these unknowns. But they lead only to unproductive guilt, which is pretty much the only kind there is. I tell her so, for my sake as much as hers. Because, sitting there in the backyard of blue hydrangea and basil and sunlight listening to her voice, all I feel is this: just sorrow. Just sorrow that we couldn't help Nick survive his addictions long enough to find a way out of them. Just sorrow that the treatment protocols and rehab centers that work for many didn't work for him. Just sorrow that Nick wanted to heal but didn't know how to make his healing last. Just sorrow that my mom (and my dad, too, every day from then until his own passing) woke up every day to this hole that has no bottom and never gets filled.

Substance addiction often involves hiding from the pain. This is true both of the person with addiction and of the people who love them and want to help them. Part of the work, therefore, is interrupting this avoidance with some honest reckoning with our feelings. Addiction thrives on shadows and hiding, on never sharing the truth of the situation even with yourself. Recovery thrives on honesty, humility, and openness with others. Which is maybe why, at the end of our conversation, when sharing words felt less necessary than sharing silence, both my mother and I feel something like relief. At least we can carry sorrow together for what we couldn't do, for what didn't work for Nick's recovery. It's not enough, but it's what we have. That's something.

When the helper can't help
A CONVERSATION WITH COURTNEY

"I'm pretty good at giving epic care!" Courtney says with a self-knowing laugh, her eyes looking up toward the ceiling of the home she shared with her husband Greg for thirty-seven years. A white, upper-middle-class woman now in her 70s, here she raised three children in a family that seemed, from the outside, a picture of success. But behind that appearance, the family was tense and torn by what Courtney describes as Greg's "lifelong love affair with alcohol." The pressure that their suburban, white-majority culture put on Courtney to hide their problems and look perfect affected how she responded to her husband's addiction.

"What's 'epic care'?" I ask, imagining superpowers of cooking and keeping watch and maintaining an unwaveringly soft, calm presence. Indeed, in the culture that Courtney and I share "care" is nearly always thought of as the work of comforting and helping others, rather than as setting limits and holding both others and ourselves accountable. "Caring" means consoling people, not challenging them to be their best selves.

"Oh, you know," she answers, "just making things easier for everyone. That's what I did, that's who I am. I take care of things, I help people, I do what I can to make them feel better. I mean, that's what I do for work, so why wouldn't I do it in every other part of my life too?"

During her marriage, Courtney worked as a nurse at a local hospital. She spent every shift responding to other people's needs, being the person who knows what to do when the buzzer buzzes and the beeper beeps and the voice calls. It's a role Courtney thrives in and is gifted at. She felt as called to nursing as any clergyperson does to ministry.

"But then I would come home and it just continued, especially when the kids were little. The housework, the homework, the laundry, the dinner, driving the kids everywhere . . ."

"And how about Greg?" I ask. "Where was Greg?"

"I mean, he was here, he was at work, whatever. But he wasn't really present, you know?"

I know, but not like Courtney knows. She is describing the "second shift" that many women work, the unpaid work inside the home that comes before and after the work that is done for money outside the home, work that some men still haven't learned to share. But Courtney also carried another burden.

"Greg's drinking just kind of crept up on me. A drink at night turned into two and three. Going to friends for dinner turned into me having to ask their help getting him into the car because he drank too much. Drinking on special occasions turned into drinking wherever we went. He would drink before we went out, then more again while we were out, and then I was the one driving home. And I just kept driving him places so he could drink. I mean, I did this for years. I was an enabler."

Courtney's eyes are cast down as she recounts all this, as if accusing herself of having done the wrong thing or not done the right one. Maybe that's why she defensively emphasizes how hard life was for her. "Every day was stressful. Every day was like being on a roller coaster. And it got to the point that what success looked like for me was just surviving the day, OK? That was enough. It's like I said to myself, 'Courtney, just take one day a time. Don't ask, can you tolerate tomorrow? Ask, can you tolerate today? And keep moving.'"

But I can see on her face how the memory still stings; how the doubt and self-judgment linger. I imagine she must wonder if she was wrong to stay with Greg for so long, instead of taking the kids and leaving when they were young. Maybe she remembers seeing dramatic interventions on television shows about addiction and thinks she should have tried one. I'm sure that, like so many people in her position, she wonders over and over again whether she truly did enough.

"Was I wrong to stay with Greg for so long? Should I have left with the kids? Should I have organized one of those interventions like you see on TV? Did I do enough?"

Courtney's eyes hold the pain of not having known what to do or how to fix things, but feeling like she should have. After a long silence of remembering, she says words that just about break my heart: "Sometimes I feel like a kind of fraud."

How can you convince someone there is no forgery or fraud in trying to love and live and nurture and parent in a home where the other partner is in a relationship with their addiction? How can you convince someone there is no version of this story where the path is clear and the choices are neat and the consequences are known? How can you convince them there is there no kind of care, no matter how "epic," that can rescue someone from their addiction if they don't want to be rescued?

Of course, Courtney knows this, but there are still times she doesn't feel it. The heart can often lead, but sometimes it can also lag. So I remind Courtney of the facts—that Greg, despite all the efforts of the people who loved him, never could find his way to recovery. That Greg denied to everyone, including himself, that he had a drinking problem. That Greg's denial was so fierce, and his desire to continue drinking so insistent, that it was hard for those who loved him to stay in relationship with him.

This was true most of all for Courtney. She spent years surviving day to day, not knowing what to do except to be as good a mother and nurse and friend as she knew how. She labored endlessly at grindingly difficult work—and yet the work she was doing is often considered ordinary, and those who do it are taken for granted. Sometimes Courtney even took herself for granted. But in the end, she decided that it was time for her to leave.

"It took a lot of courage to do that," she says, more to herself than to me. "I don't know if I could have done it when the kids were home, or if it would have been the right thing. But after a lifetime of being the person who takes care of everything and everyone, I finally realized that I couldn't fix our relationship. I couldn't fix what drove him to drinking. I couldn't make him go into recovery. But I realized the one thing I could do, the choice I still had, was to say 'I can't do this any longer.'"

If her story were a movie, there might have been a swell of redemptive music as she left. But life is much more complicated. Years later, Courtney remains both proud of her courage and pained that she needed so much of it to leave a man she loved. "That's one of the hardest parts: that I still love him. And it is because I love him that I knew I couldn't enable his drinking anymore."

———

We need to acknowledge that these stories are sad and scary. No one wants to hear that our best efforts at loving, supporting, setting limits, caretaking, intervening, praying, and persuading aren't enough to help our loved one recover from addiction. Families like mine and Courtney's, privileged enough to be used to thinking of ourselves as people who can make things happen, have an especially hard time with that truth. But the reality is that sometimes nothing more can be done to help our loved one with addiction want recovery more than they want that next drink or drug. When we reach that point, the compassion and care we've put toward them needs to be redirected back toward ourselves. Many of us never learned to nurture ourselves with the same focus and attention we gave our loved one, and we may have neglected the rest of our family in our efforts to rescue one member of it.

CHAPTER 5

What about You?

It's hard to think of self-care without thinking of the pithy one-liners we might read on a poster somewhere: Love yourself first and everything falls into place. You can't pour from an empty cup; you need to take care of yourself. Put your own oxygen mask on first. When you say "yes" to others, make sure you are not saying "no" to yourself. Self-care is not selfish. You owe yourself the love the give you give others. Taking care of yourself doesn't mean "me first"; it means "me too."

The problem with these phrases isn't that they are cliché; it's that they make us responsible for our own care. Family members of loved ones with addiction need care, too, and when the white supremacy culture we belong to tells us that we have to look after ourselves, the burden can feel overwhelming. And so we must reach out to ask for help from the people around us. It's hard and sometimes uncomfortable. But the relief it brings makes it worth it.

A grief counselor listens to the parentified child

I didn't expect to end up talking with Laura about myself or Nick or our family. She was the grief counselor on shift at the hospice center where my dad spent his final days after a fierce, brief battle with cancer, and I expected to have no more than a perfunctory chat with her.

As the oldest of three children in a family wracked by substance abuse, I have become so good at taking care of things and looking after everyone that I don't always notice my own feelings. Elaine, my therapist, has described me as a "parentified child": someone who had to become a caregiver for their family, stepping into a parental role, when they were still a child themselves. I thought I knew all about that child. I'd read the pamphlets, browsed the web pages, and paid Elaine good money to help me stop overworking and over-functioning, stop trying to meet endless responsibilities and curtail endless worries. But I was tired and raw from the days of keeping vigil, and vulnerable from the shock of my father's death. Parentified kids learn early to shield their emotions, but that day I had fewer emotional defenses than usual. So, when Laura asked about our family's story, I told her much more than I'd planned to.

We were sitting in the lobby not far from the room where my dad had died the night before. And the sharpness of the pain, of all the struggles and the dashed hopes, of my father's death and Nick's before it, surges in my heart.

"You and your family have had such a lot of loss over the last three years," she says. And that is all it takes for me to begin to cry. Sometimes we're not aware of all that we've been through and all that we're feeling until someone names it for us.

"Yeah," I mutter, wanting to meet her eyes and trying not to, all at once. And then I find myself asking, "Have you seen other families like mine?" I feel like I've been carrying all this loss alone, and I want to know if I have company.

"Oh, God, yes," she says. "Too many. Ever since opiates started getting prescribed more."

I don't know if misery always loves company, but it feels good to hear that. It feels good to know that somewhere out there is another oldest child who, like me, learned too young to anxiously look after the other people in their family. It means that somewhere out there is a club no one asks to join, whose members know what it's like to get a text from a parent that says, "please call home," and to find reasons not to because we're afraid we know what we'll find out when we do.

What's happened now? Did the rehab not work again? Mom, do you need me to call another facility? Do you want me to try calling Nick again? I was always eager, even desperate, to dive into all the work that was called for. But when you've been carrying a burden like that for years, sometimes since long before you were ready for it, it takes a toll. Some of that toll is guilt that you, the caretaker, can't seem to fix things. Some of that toll is anger at being the sibling who needs to step into the breach, again and again. And some of that toll is shame for feeling angry when everyone around you is in such pain, including you. What a cycle.

"I'm just tired," I say to Laura.

"Of course you are. Do you want to rest?"

What a question! I hadn't realized how long I'd been waiting to hear it. And immediately I burst out, "*Yes!*" And then, catching myself, "But I don't think I really know how."

What do repair and healing look like for us worriers, us anxious caretakers trying to "save" our family member from addiction? They look like the relief of discovering that we're not alone, that there are others who know exactly how it feels for us. They look like finding safe outlets for our anger, where we can express anger and love at the same time, without being judged for doing so. And they look like understanding that "saving" people like Nick isn't up to us; indeed, it never was. These are where repair and healing begin.

Loneliness in the garden

In the front of the sanctuary of the church I grew up in there was a small painting on the wall that showed Jesus in

Gethsemane, the garden where he went to pray the night before he was killed. On Sunday mornings, instead of listening to the homily, I'd lose myself in the muted colors of Jesus looking plaintively upward, asking God to somehow spare him from what was coming. At his feet were the disciples he'd asked to stay awake with him as he prayed, but who were now sprawled on the ground, sound asleep. I saw a loneliness in Jesus that I think people who love someone with addiction will understand.

Laura, the grief counselor at the hospice, runs a support group for people who have lost a family member to addiction, and when she heard about my book project she offered to connect me with some of its members. One of them is Jean, a white woman who lives in my hometown and describes herself and her family as the "working-class kind" who grow up never having quite enough.

"When it all gets too much, I just go to my garden," Jean says to me over Zoom. "It's nothing special, just some daffodils and pansies, and in the summer sometimes some cukes and tomatoes. One year I even tried to grow a pumpkin, but it didn't get real big. I don't have much space, being in the city. But it's all I—"

And her voice and face freeze there, because the internet connection is suddenly unstable. Still, I think I can complete the sentence. "It's all I've got. The garden is all I've got."

Jean lives alone these days, but not because she wants to. Her husband died from cancer a few years back. Her daughter is an active heroin user and is somewhere "out on the street." And her son Mikey died from an overdose after being released from jail.

"There was a criminal response to Mikey's use," she says. "He ended up in drug court and it became a cycle. Probation was about punishment and not recovery. I finally got him into a treatment place, and then thirty-six hours later he died, because his tolerance was lower."

The internet is back up, and Jean is clearly rocked as she recounts the wreckage of her family. Literally. Her body rocks back and forth as she tells me about each trauma, and each one visibly shakes her. It's overwhelming just listening to her.

"God, Jean," I sigh, shaking my head. And then I just look at her on the screen. In these conversations I'm learning that sometimes what's needed is more presence and fewer words. After so much destruction, silence can be comforting.

Jean breaks the quiet. "Sometimes late at night my daughter knocks on the back door, asking to come in. I give her coats, give her food, I tell her I love her, but I won't let her in unless she goes to recovery meetings with me."

"You're in recovery too?" I ask.

"Yeah, I mean, so I get it. You ever do drugs?"

I shake my head no.

"Heroin is like heaven. You have this sense that everything is okay and you're not worried about anything." She begins to cry. "I'm just brokenhearted to talk about this. I'm in recovery so I should have known, right? But when I was using and when I became a mom, I just didn't know how to make decisions. I didn't know how to accept who I was."

Isn't that the work of a lifetime, accepting who we are while also working to become the person we want to be? I wish Jean could be as full of grace with herself as she is with her children.

"I know my kids didn't do this on purpose," she says. "They have such huge hearts, but their addiction overshadowed them. But as their mom I see them as gifted, you know, as just wanting approval and love."

"Isn't it the same for you?"

And Jean's eyes look up and then well again with tears, the way our eyes often do when we hear what we already know. It's then that she brings up God.

"When Mikey died I was so mad at God; I was looking for answers and trying to find them in different religions, different beliefs. You know what I did?"

I raise my eyebrows in curiosity.

"I went to Jerusalem! I'm not even really religious, but I was looking for answers—for anything, really. The only place

I really felt something was when we went to the Garden of Gethsemane. There I felt some peace."

We take the peace where we can get it. Sometimes we find it by knowing that we're praying on the same ground where someone else prayed during their own night of trouble. Every one of us wants to know who will stay awake and keep watch with us. No wonder that, when it all gets to be too much, Jean continues to go to her garden.

Learning to confide in others

Never mind living and thriving; sometimes just surviving is the goal. Did we get through the day without any major blow-ups? Did I get to work on time? Did the kids get to school? Do I know where my loved one is? Do I know they are safe? Sometimes getting answers to these questions takes so much energy that we can scarcely notice how we are feeling.

Shellie knows about all this. For more than twenty years she lived in the shadow of her husband's alcoholism while raising three children and working full time to support the family.

"After all those years of parenting, working, and keeping the house together, just surviving was a success. I spent so much energy making things look okay on the outside and for everyone else that I just lost touch with myself. It was like the house was there, but there was no foundation."

Putting out all that energy took a toll on her. "Everything got reduced down into sort of tiny, manageable bites—errands, tasks, getting the basics done in spite of my husband's increasing unreliability as a parent and partner. My world just got smaller and smaller. And then I got small. I felt so confined."

Shellie is a strong, accomplished white, middle-class woman and a loving parent, but eventually she hit her limit. It happened when one of her children began to struggle at school and she knew she didn't have the emotional resources to help. This need to reach beyond her smallness and isolation led Shellie to therapy and then to a meeting of Al-Anon, a mutual support program for people whose lives have been affected by someone else's drinking. It was there that something happened for Shellie that hadn't happened in years: someone else asked her how she was.

"At first I didn't even know what to say. But as I heard others share and listened to how their experience mirrored my own, it was like I began to feel again. I realized that one way I had coped with my husband's drinking and all the chaos it brought was to go numb, to kind of tune out my emotions because it was just too painful, too scary."

When the gates of emotion opened and Shellie began to take notice of herself, she was surprised that the first feeling she discovered was shame. "Shame that I didn't give myself attention. Shame that I had let myself go so far into the background. Shame that I hadn't modeled self-care for my children. But when I reported this to my friends in Al-Anon they caught me. They said it was time I stopped blaming the victim, which was me. They caught me before I started going inward—silencing myself, guilting myself, making myself feel small again."

Shellie's husband is still going in and out of recovery, but Shellie herself has recovered from living in an alcoholic family system. "How I gauge my recovery these days is to what degree my life feels expansive, feels open. Am I able to check in with myself? Am I putting myself in places where self-reflection is expected? Am I making time to connect with those people who ask how I am and have the time to actually listen? When I do these things I remember it's not in my power to 'fix' my spouse, but what is in my power is to give myself appropriate self-regard."

Shellie's example leaves us with important takeaways. We need to find places and people, such as Al-Anon or another support group, who share our experiences of living in a family system of addiction. We need to trust these people enough to tell them how we truly are, without pretense. And we need to hear them when they remind us that we can and should do more than just survive our loved one's addiction; we should give ourselves the self-regard we need and deserve.

Remembering joy

Remember joy? Remember the feeling of lightness that comes when we're laughing over dinner with family or friends, or catching up on some soothingly bad television, or retreating into a good book, or taking the time to treat ourselves to something we love? When so much of our energy is used up responding to the actions of our loved one with addiction, making time and space to do things we enjoy can seem impossible. And anyway, how do we enjoy anything when we're not feeling particularly joyful?

"Yeah, I get all that," says my therapist Elaine. "Do the things you love anyway. Very often the practice of joy comes first and the feeling of joy comes later." She tells me that doing things that make us happy and give us joy is like physical therapy for the soul. Doctors don't prescribe bed rest anymore, because they know that the body needs to move in order to recover. So do our emotions. The parts of us that know how to laugh and smile and play—our "joy muscles"—don't get much exercise when we're caught up with fret and fear because our loved one is struggling. But we need to free ourselves of that emotional tangle, to step back and get some distance and perspective. And nothing helps us do that so well as doing something we love—even if we don't feel like doing it. Will the same worries be there when we return? Of course. But we won't be the same. We return at least a little refreshed, a little more focused, a little less overwhelmed, a little less "heavy." It's not exactly a new beginning, but it is something like renewal.

Do things that make you proud

"I can't remember the last time I felt proud," Mark, a white, middle-class dad in his late 40s, tells me. "Trying to figure out what to do about my son's drug use and not having any real answers caused me to get pretty down on myself. I mean, I'm his dad. Aren't I supposed to know what to do? Isn't that what a parent is?"

Mark needed a way to get his confidence back, to be reminded that he was better than he believed. Fortunately, he accepted an invitation to mentor one of our congregation's youth in a yearlong class called "Coming of Age." He initially doubted that he had anything to offer another teenager when his own child was struggling so much. But meeting weekly to go over the class's themes and how they related to this young person's life gave him the opportunity to remember that he is actually a pretty good listener and gentle advice-giver.

"I had just gotten so accustomed to feeling like nothing I did was working as a father, which made the dynamic with my son even worse. But over that year I got some of my self-respect back. I remembered that I actually have a lot to give and that I can be a pretty good dad. What was amazing was to see how mentoring this other teen actually helped me parent my own teen, because it reminded me of what I'm good at. I started listening to my son again. I checked my defensiveness. I expressed my worries about him with soft directness rather than blowing up. I felt reenergized."

Not everyone can do it, or wants to, but for some of us sharing our gifts outside of ourselves and our immediate family is a tremendous help in reminding us that we are more than the role we play in responding to our loved one's addiction. In whatever way is right for us, we need to find things to do that help us remember that we are more than the guilt, self-doubt, and helplessness that haunt every friend and family member of someone who is suffering with addiction.

Know your limits

When my mother and I spoke about how it was for her and my dad in the last months of Nick's life, she mentioned a coping strategy that caught my ear.

"When things got bad with Nick, he had this habit of just calling me all the time. He was just so desperate and scared, and I had always been the person he reached out to when he felt that way, even when he was little. But he would call all the time, and—"

And here I could hear her voice cracking with emotion, the memory stinging.

"And, I hate to admit this, but there were times when I would hear the phone ring and see on the caller ID that it was him and I would just let it ring. There were times I wouldn't pick up. I just couldn't, you know? Because I didn't have the patience, or the energy, and I knew I would say something I would regret."

And then she said something key. "I also knew it wasn't good for me—or for him, for that matter—to keep going in circles together, talking and talking about the same problems: me giving the same advice, him telling me why it wouldn't work, and then circling back to the beginning again. So I let his calls go to voicemail sometimes, because I knew I was at my limit.

"Do you think I did the right thing?" That is a painful question that all of us who have tried to balance caring for ourselves and caring for a loved one in need have likely asked. "Do you think it's okay that I didn't answer when he called?"

Yes, it's okay. My mom knew that to answer Nick's call in those moments would have required her to give more than she had, and that talking wasn't what either of them needed then. But what a heartrending balance to have to strike—this balance between wanting more than anything else to respond to your child's desperation, and knowing that doing so isn't good for either of you.

Shellie tells me at the end of our conversation that she is learning to care for herself and her children in a home with addiction by reminding herself, "I can't give out of my essence; I can only give out of my abundance." For Shellie, and for all of us who are trying to figure out how to care for ourselves and our families, giving out of our abundance rather than our essence means creating some emotional space between ourselves and the worry and work engendered by our loved one's addiction.

The practices highlighted here—finding others we can share our experience with, doing things we enjoy, doing things that make us feel proud and empowered, and knowing our limits—are all ways we can reconnect with our abundance, even in the midst of the work that is involved in loving someone in the throes of substance addiction. Even though that work so often seems to deplete our essence. And these practices are made much easier by the support and empathy that comes from community. We can't just give ourselves the care we need. We need and deserve the same attention we are giving to our loved one with addiction, and it can only come from others. There is relief in learning that we are held in others' care.

CHAPTER 6

What about the Rest of Your Family?

I was cleaning out a drawer one day and found a family photograph from when my siblings and I were kids. It's from one of those amusement park rides that captures you mid-scream, on that edge between thrill and fear, and then charges $10 to have it printed out and stuck in a flimsy cardboard frame. I sat on the floor and got lost in our faces, imagining what each of us must have been thinking and feeling. Oh no! Look at that drop! Will this safety bar hold? Will I be OK? Can someone hold my hand?

Years later, addiction would take us on another kind of ride. Nick was the one who was using, but it's not as though the rest of were just onlookers, saying, "You go ahead; we'll just wait for you here." Our whole family was riding with him, each of us affected in different ways. That's the thing about loving someone with addiction. The addiction doesn't just involve them. It's a family affair.

Taking care of business

"I had all these plans for retirement someday," says Tricia. "You know how you have these pictures in your mind? I had water in mind, and trips far away."

There is a long pause, long enough for me to wonder if our call has dropped. "Tricia, you there?"

"Yeah, here," she says, her voice cracking with emotion. "But now I just put my head down and take care of business. Failure isn't an option. My mom raised me to survive."

It's been three years since Tricia's twenty-eight-year-old daughter died from an overdose on her front porch. The police left her body there for hours while they investigated for "criminal activity," a callous act of disrespect that Tricia says had everything to do with her Black skin and her Black neighborhood. "The police only started to treat this problem of drugs differently when white people started showing up overdosing in the ER."

Tricia's daughter left three children under the age of ten. Instead of planning for retirement, now Tricia is saving for her grandchildren's college educations and waking every morning at 4 a.m. to pack their lunches and make them breakfast before school. "I'm their mom now," she says, as much to herself as to me. "My old life is gone. These kids are mine."

As a minister, I can normally keep my emotions in check, focusing on the person I'm with rather than on my reactions to them. But by the time Tricia and I talk I've spent so much time with so many people carrying such unbearable loss that my emotions are spilling over all my edges. This time I'm overflowing with sadness, and a longing to be able to just step through the phone line and sit with her. After so many years carrying my own loss mostly alone, I crave these connections.

Tricia met my mom at a weekend retreat for mothers who have lost children to substance abuse. If it weren't for their shared experience, Tricia and I would never have met. Our neighborhoods, our races, our upbringings segregate us. If there is an upside to any of this, it is the connection, the kinship, that comes from sharing pain.

Now she is asking about my mom. "How is she? We chatted all weekend long at the retreat. We've been meaning to get lunch."

"Oh, you know," I say, "somewhere in the middle." Somewhere in the middle between good days and bad, between love and longing, between the sting of loss and the relief that she doesn't have to worry about Nick anymore. That is how it is for families like ours. As we were in that amusement park photo, we're feeling many things at once.

"Me too," Tricia says. "Lately I've been tangling most with the oldest child. She's twelve. She keeps wanting to blame her mom's absence every time she gets in trouble at school. I tell her, 'If I can't use this as an excuse, neither can you! She was my daughter much longer than she was your mom!'" Tricia's voice is a mixture of frustration and compassion. What she says is true, but it's also true that her granddaughter is just a kid who has lost her mom.

"It's hardest on her and the other, who is ten. The youngest, at six, doesn't remember a whole lot about his mom. But the oldest two have all sorts of memories. Their dad was a drug user too, and they both just have so much shame when they get asked about their parents. What do I tell them? I don't know what to tell them."

But that's not entirely true. Later she remarks that she sees telling the kids about their mom as one of her primary jobs. "I tell them stories from when she was a child, how silly she was, how big her heart was. I want them to know more about her than those last years when the addiction got ahold of her."

In the same way, I want to know and remember more about Nick—and, it needs to be said, about my dad, too, whose own drinking got out of control after Nick died. And about my mom, who was a steadfast wife and mother through it all (and who surely, like Tricia, gave up a lot). And about my younger sister, who, like me, has too often been called on to care for the family. I want to see a fuller picture of who we all are, separate and together, and not just a frozen image of us mid-trauma, grabbing for a safety bar on the ride that addiction has taken us on.

I want this most when I preach. One of Unitarian Universalism's parent traditions is a Christian theology of universal salvation, and while modern Unitarian Universalism is not a Christian denomination and does not hold that we need to be "saved" from any eternal fate, we cherish and preach our belief that human beings are fundamentally good, that each of us has inherent worth and dignity. Our theology draws from our Universalist heritage to promise that everyone deserves a second chance, that everyone deserves and can achieve healing. But before Nick's death, I could preach this message without actually wrestling with the challenge it sets out. Now sometimes I can live out that theology, and sometimes I can't. In his book *Tattoos on the Heart*, Gregory Boyle, a Catholic priest, says, "God is just too busy loving us to have any time left for disappointment," but I am not God, and sometimes I'm too busy being disappointed in Nick to remember to love him.

"It's hard for me to say this out loud," Tricia says, "but she let me down. You know what I mean? You ever feel that way about your brother?"

"Uh-huh." I've never spoken about this so clearly and directly before, but I tell Tricia how let down I feel by the fact that he isn't here to share things with me. He missed my son's, his nephew's, graduation from high school. He never was able to send a card for my twentieth wedding anniversary. He missed his own son's first day of kindergarten. He missed the vigils at our dad's hospice bed. He couldn't help me write the eulogy at our dad's funeral. He isn't around to help me check up on our mom week after week. I feel both ashamed and relieved to admit that sometimes I just want to snap, "Damn it, Nick!"

Through the phone I feel Tricia nodding. Kinship. "How about you?" I ask, and her own disappointment is clear as well.

"I gave up everything for her, I worked, I was a single mom. Did I give her too much of things she wanted? Did I rescue her too much? Did I enable her? Sometimes I feel betrayed because of all the effort that went into raising her and helping her get on her feet. And I'm not alone. She had a caseworker from DSS [the Department of Social Services] who was there to give her whatever help she needed. But she just wouldn't take it, or she couldn't. It [the addiction] really had a hold on her. She was a loving mom. Her kids were her world. But in the last few years I could just feel her drifting further and further away."

I recognize the resignation in her voice, because I share it. Nick was the same way, similar enough to Tricia's daughter for me to feel shocked but not surprised when he overdosed. I hadn't given up on his recovery so much as accepted that I was powerless to change his trajectory. It was and is a terrible acceptance. Tricia felt it, too.

"I feel like I did all I could do, you know? But I was so stressed out caring for my grandkids that I couldn't do anything more. My mom was different, though. Sometimes I think she suffered the biggest impact. She never gave up on my daughter. She always gave her what she wanted. For sure she enabled her. And now she's got this guilt that won't let her go."

Repair

As a Unitarian Universalist, I believe that redemption and healing are available to all. Not all UUs believe in God or have a practice they would call "prayer," but I do—and yet sometimes my prayers sound like requests to help my unbelief. I think this is because my trauma is deeply rooted within me, and easily triggered. It's not as bad as it used to be, but I still can't feel the buzz of my phone without worrying that it brings bad news. Elaine, my therapist, tells me this is to be expected and encourages me to check my fear against reality. "Aren't the calls sometimes just spam? Couldn't it be someone you know who got a new phone number?"

Her promptings are annoying, but only because they remind me how much my family's addiction experience has narrowed my ability to see beyond the trauma it caused me.

"Healing," she tells me, "looks like you practicing to not assume the worst when you get an unexpected call. And you know what else?"

Whenever she says this, I know something hard is coming.

"Healing looks like you remembering your brother for more than his last years of life, when his addiction was raging."

I contemplate finding a new therapist who won't ask me to do hard things. I'm paying them, right? Instead, I practice spending time with memories of Nick that help me remember more of him—like when I taught him to do a backflip on our trampoline when we were kids, and in return he taught me how to do the moonwalk (he was quite the dancer). The time when, years later, he asked me to officiate at his wedding, and I led him line by line through his vows after he became too emotional to say them unprompted. The time when he called me to say, voice bursting with elation, that he was going to be a dad and wanted my advice about the best stroller to buy.

"One priority," I told him. "Make sure it has a place to hold your coffee."

I feel better when I remember Nick's wholeness like this. I need the reality check, the reminders that he was more than his addiction. I suspect this is how God sees us and how we can see each other: the joy mixing with pain, the light with the shadow.

I tell all this to Tricia, because I've learned that another thing that heals is talking with someone who understands.

"She was my baby," Tricia declares, then corrects herself: "No, she *is* my baby. I'm supposed to take care of my baby. After she died, I had a hard time accepting it was real. The only thing that helped was putting together the funeral, because it made it real. It was also one way I could still take care of her. So that's what helps me move forward now, taking care of my baby. And the only way I know how to take care of my daughter is to take care of her babies."

One night the youngest one woke everyone up at 4 a.m., screaming. He had fallen out of bed and broken his arm. "What I wanted to do was just go back to bed and pull the covers over my head, you know? But the only way I can take care of my child now is to take care of her children. So I scooped him up and took him to the clinic to get a cast, and then I went in for my full day of work."

It's exhausting, but Tricia finds purpose in it. "Now I need to take care of my daughter in a different way. Now I'm in a mode where I have to take care of business, and the business is these children. They are mine now. It doesn't help me move on, but it does help me move forward. You get the difference, right?"

"Oh, yes," I say. I get that repair does not mean fixing the past or putting the past out of our sight. Instead, it means learning to live with the changes the past has dealt.

Several days after we speak, Tricia texts me to ask if I would like to read the poem she wrote for her daughter's funeral. "Writing is a way I'm using to process my grief. It is truer now than when I wrote it. Maybe you can put it in the book?"

Yes, I can, Tricia. Here it is:

A piece of my heart is missing;
through these tears I cannot see,
A piece of my heart is missing, torn away from me . . .
blown in the wind, strewn like autumn leaves,
scattered like golden sand about an ocean beach.
A piece of my heart is missing, never to be replaced.
A piece of my heart is missing;
may she rest in God's loving grace.
Mommy loves you forever and always.

CHAPTER 7

Come Out of Hiding, Come into Community

A Family Testimony

It had been years since I had talked with Taylor. The last time I remembered seeing him was a Sunday after worship, when he told me that his high school basketball practice schedule would probably keep him from coming on Sundays or to youth group. "So you won't see me much, but I'm cool, Nathan, I'm good," he said. Which was true . . . until it wasn't. The next year I learned from his parents that Taylor was using heroin.

How did this happen? Taylor? The little kid from a middle-class white family with the sideways smile I'd see on Sunday mornings before worship, the one who was often my foil during the children's sermon, who attended religious education classes for his whole childhood? Yes, that Taylor, because addiction has no boundaries, touches all zip codes, finds root in all kinds of families, runs ragged and raging in all kinds of people.

And as I've said, "why?" isn't the most important question. The most important question is how it is that Taylor is standing before me on this autumn Sunday morning, having been in recovery for eighteen months. "Nathan, great to see you!" he beams, giving me a full two-armed hug. "When am I talking in the service?" He will be introducing the executive director of the recovery program that has helped him get and stay clean, the recipient of this morning's offering. I pull out the order of service to show him the details, and as he takes it in his hands I think about all that those hands must have held, these last years. The drugs, yes, but also the pamphlets explaining recovery houses. His family's front door handle, each time he came home. Maybe he put his head in his hands, rubbing his temples, during the hurting, hating moments in detox. Certainly he handled his train pass every day, going into the city for recovery meetings, and his phone during long talks with his sponsor. Imagining all that Taylor has been through these last years brings me closer to him, nurtures my empathy for him, helps me to open the doors of my heart wider to him. This is important because it is so easy to be angry with the people addiction claims, to blame them and feel disappointed in them, as though they are making a free choice to hurt themselves and the people who love them rather than also being victimized by the drug, the drink, the pull to use.

Taylor has just gotten a text. "Oh, man," he says. "Looks like Charlie got his directions wrong."

"Charlie, the executive director, the one who you are supposed to introduce and who is supposed to do most of the talking?"

"Yeah."

"OK, hmmm. What do you want to do?" I know Taylor is nervous about getting up in front of all these people. "You want me to do the talking instead? I'm happy—"

But Taylor interrupts, "Nah, I got it. It's fine. I'll do it. I'm cool, Nathan, I'm good."

Which was true . . . and this time, it stayed true. Because when the time came to introduce the offering, Taylor stood up from the pew where he was sitting near his parents and stepped forward into the pulpit, nerves and conviction and poise mixing together as he brought the microphone to his lips. He looked into the eyes of the congregation, many of whom had known him since he was a child, took a breath, and began to speak.

It didn't take long for me to notice the impact of his words. I heard the hush, I felt the silence, I saw the tears well as Taylor told us how he had grown up in this church, sat in that pew, was taught by this teacher, mentored by that adult, mumbled along with these hymns, even paid attention to some sermons. And how today was his first time back in years.

"I'm an addict," Taylor said, without shame. He described his experience of addiction to us, driving home how it isn't something that only happens to other people, in other places. Addiction is here among people we know: our teens, our parents, our coworkers, our church community.

"I spent a long time in denial, you know? But maybe that's the same for you, too. It's really hard to face the reality that addiction is everywhere . . . man, it's everywhere! But that's why I'm up here today, to tell the truth. That's what church is for, right? Isn't that what we're about?"

While Taylor spoke, I kept an eye on his parents. Sarah and Rob were sitting together on the right side of the sanctuary, up against the windows. Before this moment of Taylor's public truth-telling only a handful of people in the congregation had known about his addiction. Now everyone did. What was that like? What were they feeling?

———

"I remember hearing the heating turn on," says Sarah. "It was so quiet when he spoke. The silence was palpable."

"I could hear my ears ringing," says Rob.

The only people at church that Sarah had confided in about Taylor's addiction were the other members of her spiritual discussion and support group. "I just blurted it out one time during check-in. I didn't plan on it. I was just under so much stress."

"I told a couple of the church band members," says Rob. "But I kept it pretty low-key because . . . I mean, what could I say?"

Sarah, Rob, and I are sitting at their kitchen table. It's been more than two years since that Sunday when Taylor spoke, almost four since he fell into addiction, but as soon as I invite them to remember his active addiction and the early days of recovery they are as present as if they had been yesterday. Trauma does that. The memories stay fresh, perhaps forever.

"Up until that moment I felt like I was hiding. I was in the shadows. Most people in my life didn't know," Sarah says. "Once it became clear what was really going on with him, that he was using heroin—"

Rob interrupts: "You called me at work, remember? You said, 'I just found out Taylor is using heroin. Can you come home?'"

"Oh, right, yes. That was horrible. And so once it became clear, once we knew what was really happening, and Taylor finally went into recovery, I remember I would literally hide in the grocery store, because our town is not a big town. Everyone knows each other. I just felt like all eyes were on me. I'm sure I overestimated that . . . but I remember a lot of situations where everyone's like, 'my child is doing this or that great thing,' and I'm just thinking, 'well, mine was in a hospital last month and now he's in a recovery house.' I just felt this stigma, this shame."

For Sarah the memory still stings, and even though Rob is more quiet, his downcast eyes and slow nod say the same for him. So what was it like to have Taylor tell everyone in their community the truth? What was it like to break the cultural expectation that we should keep our struggles private? Did the shame just get worse?

Sarah says no. "Remember, by that time we been going to support groups for families going through the same stuff, so I got used to outing myself many times. But when Taylor got up there and began to speak, you know what the biggest thing I felt was? It was relief."

"Yeah," Rob chimes in. "Because finally we didn't have to figure out who knew at church anymore, or what kind of conversations we could have, or have to explain it all a thousand times. It was a relief, yeah, a big relief."

"And what about after? What did people say to you?"

"Oh, I mean . . . I don't even remember!" says Sarah. "Isn't that interesting? I mean, I think I remember awkward conversations in coffee hour because some folks, most folks, just don't know what to say after hearing something like that."

Rob adds, "I wasn't really looking for anything from anyone. I didn't need any special outreach or support from the whole church. We had other places for that, OK? But I guess it just felt good, finally, that everyone knew."

"Yeah, because this is our community and it's just a relief to be real here."

———

When we welcome new members into our congregation, the covenant we share with them asks for their help in building a community that is real and makes room for each person to show up without pretense. The covenant's words are lovely and inspired, but they are also only words. Taylor's lasting gift to our community—and also to his parents—was to show us what it means to be real. We are embedded in white supremacy culture, which drives us to perfectionism and makes us see ourselves as failures when, inevitably, we fall short of being perfect. Taylor's sharing, without pretense or shame, has enabled others to do the same. I watched it happen. First one person asked for an appointment with me, and then another, and soon a small group were telling their stories of addiction and seeking the help they needed. By breaking with the cultural expectation that struggles should be hidden, Taylor showed us that stories like his and his family's need to be brought out into the open air. Only in a caring community, whether a religious congregation, a support group, or some other kind, can we get the practical and emotional support we need.

But as a minister, I believe that communities of faith, in particular, offer powerful resources for those struggling with

addiction and their loved ones. When addiction brings isolation and despair, a congregation says, "Come, gather, sing,
cry, talk, worship, tell the truth, be real." And as a Unitarian
Universalist, I believe that our great principle of the worth
and dignity of every person, without exception, counters
addiction's drive to blame and shame. All are worthy; all are
welcome. In a culture that tells us to hide our stories of addiction, true spiritual community reminds us that everyone is
struggling in some way, and we should share each other's pain.
When we are exhausted and consumed by worry for someone
we love who is in the throes of addiction, congregations hold
hope for us.

And so, Taylor: thank you.

Conclusion

About four years ago, I began to open every sermon I gave to my congregation with these words from Leonard Cohen's song "Anthem":

> "Forget your perfect offering.
> There is a crack in everything;
> That's how the light gets in."

It didn't occur to me until I began writing this book that the timing wasn't a coincidence. I heard another preacher begin a sermon this way only a few months after my brother died, and I immediately felt drawn to the lines. They expressed how I felt as someone whose love, prayers, attention, focus, and advice ultimately weren't enough to save his brother from his addictions. I have had to give up the idea that my family or I could have offered him any kind of "perfect" solution. I have learned more about living with grief than I ever imagined I would, and I've been cracked open by loss and humility.

Have those cracks allowed light to get in? I get angry when people try to brush away terrible events by pointing to any good thing they can claim came out of the tragedy, as though that made it worth it. I have learned a lot about myself, others, and addiction as a result of my brother's overdose death, but I would give it all up in a second if I could have him back. But because I can't, I have needed to look for the light that the subsequent years of learning about addiction and listening to people's stories have allowed in.

Some rays of that light have been the conversations presented in this book. Nearly all of the people I spoke with were members or friends of the Unitarian Universalist Area Church in Sherborn, Massachusetts, or were connected to the congregation in some way. I have changed names and some personal details, but all the tender, painful, complex, unresolved, and sometimes hopeful experiences presented here were ones I heard during hours of honest conversation. Some people told me that our conversation was the first time they had talked with anyone about the impact that addiction has had on their family. It's a painful reminder of just how much the white supremacy culture of perfectionism and individualism has affected us all. And it reminds me, in particular, that Unitarian Universalists must continue centering the spiritual values of interdependence and empathy in our congregations, so that more families will feel they can come to us for care.

Another ray of that light, of course, is this book and however it may companion you as you live with your loved one with addiction. We never stop asking how and why addiction happens, what we can do to help, what we can't do, and how to care for ourselves and our family in the midst of it all. I know I have been helped by hearing how other people have tried to answer these questions. I pray that you will be, too.

A third and different kind of ray has been my deeper awareness of the role that social location and race play in how we respond to substance use and abuse in our communities. My conversations with Rev. Lloyd made the importance of these factors especially apparent to me, and I began to see that many of my assumptions about addiction were rooted in the white supremacy culture that my congregation, my family, and I are embedded in. Rev. Lloyd's invitation to spiritually "tarry with folk" rather than "run or shun" was one I had longed to hear and now want to extend. We often spend too long trying to figure out the "perfect" response to those in our community who have a family member with addiction or who are struggling with addiction themselves, and we work too hard to keep those responses personal and private, failing to examine our cultural assumption that addiction is something to be ashamed of and kept secret. But as Rev. Lloyd observed, "Addiction never just happens to the individual. It happens to the community." As a minister I am called to ask how my faith community can best respond to families who are struggling. And I have learned that an important part of my ministry is to make public what we have for too long kept private. The Unitarian Universalist values of covenant and community can be strong counters to the pressure toward shame and secrecy.

Working on this book has helped me grow, but the thing about growth is that it often hurts. Listening to these stories, exploring my own, and writing it all down has at times been bruising. I have often wanted to do anything but sit down and get to writing. But recovery begins when we lean into, rather than away from, the fact that the disease of addiction has struck our family and begin to grapple with what to do about it. I hope that this book will be part of that recovery, for me and for you.

Acknowledgments

Interviewing for and writing this book has been a rich and challenging process. I want to thank everyone who shared their addiction experiences with me with such willingness and vulnerability, particularly when these experiences haven't been talked about often or at all. This includes some of my own family members, who shared more fully about the impact addiction has had on them than any time in our relationship.

I am also grateful for the support, affirmation, and time given me to work on this project by the members and friends of the Unitarian Universalist Area Church at First Parish in Sherborn, Massachusetts, including a five-month sabbatical and regular cheerleading to keep me going through all the necessary edits and additions.

Speaking of edits, this book simply wouldn't exist without the thoughtful, committed guidance of Mary Bernard at Skinner House, who walked with me from the very beginning of this project through its completion and encouraged and challenged me when I needed it most.

Last, deep gratitude to my family—my spouse Karyn and children Emerson and Ella—who never missed the chance to remind me of the commitment I made after my brother's death, which was to take my grief and turn it into something that could be a resource for those who are struggling to love someone with addiction. Their expressions of love, comfort and "Get back to writing!" are what helped me keep my commitment every step of the way.

Recovery and Support Programs

Al-Anon   **al-anon.org**

Alcoholics Anonymous   **aa.org**

Narcotics Anonymous   **na.org**

Adult Children of Alcoholics   **adultchildren.org**

UU Addictions Ministry   **uuaddictionsministry.org**